Now That's Riddle-Culous!
Tricky Riddles for Adults
(Second Edition)

A letter from The Chocokola Guy!

First I would like to thank you for purchasing this book.

Let me introduce myself, I am the one and only, The Chocokola guy, I am your half-dude, half-koala friend who makes a living by being a NINJA by day and wrestling giant hippos at night.

I live inside a giant red mushroom with my mom and dad, and we eat honey and milk all day.

When we're not doing anything, we watch TV, and we play outside with our pet dinosaur.

Thanks for training your mind one tricky riddle at a time

Riddle on!

The Chocokola Guy

Japanese People's Mental Game Secret

Heyya!

Please DO me a favor, for the next two minutes, don't laugh at this TECHNIQUE and take this advice seriously.

Deal? Great!

Did you know that the Japanese actually did a research with 132 students (which they grouped in 2) and they asked the STUDENTS to undergo a series of Tasks and Tests which are originally DESIGNED to stress people out!

Such as:

- Operations: A task where you'll need to avoid LIVEWIRES while moving your arms and legs away...

- Finding the next number on a series...(sounds easy, but it isn't!)

After the first group was done...

The other half of the students were ASKED to do this...

"STARE AND GAZE" at cute baby animal images! (for several minutes...)

And then they were asked to take the same tasks...

Guess what happened...

To their surprise...the results they had trampled the first group by a whopping 44% !

Which means for every 10 seconds the first group took to do something, the 2nd group only took 6.6 seconds to do the same task!

The scientists believed that this is due to the increased visual and mental acuity after looking at things which has a "baby schema" or simply to say...

...creatures that portray the features of a baby! (huge forehead and eyes, small nose...etc)

Now...

What are you waiting for

Search for cute kitties now online!

Table of Content

Introduction

The fantastic thing with the human brain is its ability to adapt to things around it. This is the reason why people are able to do such amazing mental and physical feats.

Those things that people thought to be impossible until done!

However, the thing with the brain is that it needs practice and mastery before it can perform amazing feats.

Just like an unstoppable surging flame, the brain is majestic itself, but it needs some spark, to begin with.

To achieve real and long-lasting greatness, you need to fan the little embers of knowledge inside you.

No matter the size, if you have the will to let that little spark consume you, then you have a great shot.

One way to get things started with training your mind is answering logical questions!

The power of these difficult brain teasers is sure to push you to the edges of your mind because answering these types of puzzles requires a lot of out-of-the-box thinking.

Perfect for teens, adults and super brilliant kids!

Excellent Mind Training – Great way to train and expand your mind

Awesome with Friends– Team up with your friends and families and enjoy cracking these brain teasers together

Develop Your Lateral Thinking –Develop your confidence in solving real-life problems by practicing here!

Improve Vocabulary and Comprehension – Learn new amazing words and concepts about the world!

Surprise Interview Questions – Some of these questions are actually used at job interviews and scholarship applications!

Why answer these difficult riddles anyway?

Learn Various Approaches to Problems. One of the most crucial skills in life that one can learn is the ability to answer and look at problems with different perspectives and approaches.

There is no universal approach to all the questions in the world, and that is where these riddles come for help. These riddles require different approaches to be answered.

Save Your Time by Constant Learning. Whenever we try to answer a problem at hand, it is not always the actual problem that makes it difficult to answer, but rather the unnecessary information that comes with it.

When answering these difficult riddles, one must learn to pay attention only to the essential facts.

Develop Empathy. We've only got one planet to live with, but don't make the mistake to think that all of us are living in the same world.

Every single person on this entire planet are living with different worldviews, beliefs, and brain patterns, the reason being is this; it is because all of us live with unfathomable variables, to begin with.

We may never understand every single idea there is out there, and honestly, we do not have to. The only important thing is that we learn to accept different ideologies and concepts, and that skill itself is a direct effect of answering logical questions.

Figuring out these riddles requires you to open up yourself to the abstract and the uncommon.

Enhance Your Communication Skills. In order to deliver your "proposals" and "theories" to the world, you must know your stuff first, the others will soon follow.

When you know your stuff well, then you can do a better job conveying yourself.

Transform Your Decision Making Skills. It is incredible to think how much energy and time one can save when logical and critical thinking is applied to the situation.

The moment we decide to leave the guesswork behind outside the door, we open up ourselves to better and sounder decisions.

Improve Your Reasoning. There are two primary types of reasoning people use, (we may not be aware of it, but there is indeed such a thing!) Inductive and deductive reasoning.

Perfect Navigation

This book is specifically designed for you and your device. Not only did we take our time coming up with all these riddles, but we also took good efforts in making your experience the best as you navigate through this book.

Table of Content

Go to your Favorite Riddle every single time by checking the page on the Table of Content.

The Answers

You can easily see if your answer is correct by looking at the end of each riddle.

Some of the answers are pretty long, and some aren't...most will make perfect sense and some won't.

I hope that you burn some time along using this book!

World's Best Difficult Riddles!

"Difficult times is what brings out the best in people."

Bernie Sanders

Riddle 1: The Mystery Boat

There is a docked mysterious boat beside a lake with a ladder hanging off in its side.

The ladder has 10 rungs, which each of these rungs has a 12-inch separation from one to another.

The lake was calm that day, and the high tide is starting to kick in, whereas the water level rises by about 4 inches per hour.

The question is, how many hours will it take for the 3rd rung to be submerged into the lake?

Answer:

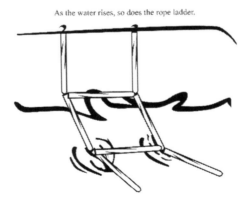

As the water rises, so does the rope ladder.

The water will never reach the 3rd rung, because as the water level rises, so does the boat itself!

Riddle 2: Used Uselessly

It's useless when it is used. Once offered, it's always rejected.

In desperation often expressed!

What am I?

Answer:

A poor alibi / a weak excuse!

Riddle 3: A Chemist's Mystery

A long time ago, there was a very successful chemist who was kidnapped.

A note written on a piece of paper by the victim was found, which is as follows:

26-3-58 / 28-27-57-16'

With this note, the police have narrowed down the search and identified that two persons did the crime.

Here are their possible suspects:

Nicolas, Adam, Felice, Steven, Condriano, Paul

Who among these are the killers?

Answer:

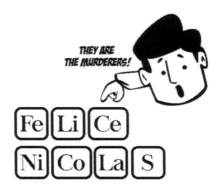

Felice and Nicholas are the kidnappers. The numbers written are the atomic numbers of the elements, which is 'Fe-Li-Ce/Ni-Co-La-S' on the periodic table!

Riddle 4: Mortal Privation

Reminding man of mortal privation, when set in place.

The everlasting summation tattooed on my face.

What am I?

Answer: A Tombstone

Riddle 5: Proverb Word Play

The letters in each of the sentences below are all mixed up, and if jumbled correctly, these are actually some FAMOUS proverbs / sayings!

Can you identify their original sentences?

1. I don't admit women are faint.

2. It rocks. The broad flag of the free.

3. Strong lion's share almost gone.

Answer:

1. Time and tide wait for no man.

2. Birds of a feather flock together.

3. A rolling stone gathers no moss.

Riddle 6: Scent

Even after smelling me, buying me, and delivering me, I will never ever change.

What three words am I?

Answer: Scent, Cent, Sent

Riddle 7: Homeostasis

A natural state sought by all.

Go without me, and you shall fall.

You need me when you spend,

And you meet me after eating with no END!

What am I?

Answer: Balance

Riddle 8: Friends

Suppose you are a ship captain and you just rescued a lot of survivors from a remote island.

In the ship, one of the survivors asked your crew for 1/2 cup of water and the next person asked for 1/4 cup of water, then the next survivor asked for 1/8 cup of water, and the sequence goes on and on.

How many cups of water does your crew have to give to all of the survivors if they will continue to ask you for water in this sequence?

Answer: Just 1 Cup is enough. If the survivors kept asking for water like this forever, one cup would be enough.

Riddle 9: Who Am I?

What person is he that builds stronger structures than a mason, a shipwright, or even a carpenter?

Answer: The gravedigger, for his houses will last forever!

Riddle 10: Cups of Coffee

You have a cup of tea (T) and a cup of coffee (C), which has equal amounts. You took a spoonful of the coffee (C) and mix it thoroughly into the tea (T).

After mixing, you take a spoonful from the cup of tea (T) you just mixed the spoonful of coffee with earlier, and you put it in the cup of coffee (C).

Does the cup which initially had tea in it (T) have more coffee or does the cup that initially had coffee in it (C) have more tea?

Answer:

Both cups will end up having the same amount of the other liquid in it because when you transfer the spoonful of coffee (C) and put it in the tea (A), it increases the volume of the tea (T) by that spoonful.

When you transfer a spoonful of the tea (A), part of that spoonful is coffee, taking away the proportional amount of coffee. With this, it makes the amount of coffee in the tea and tea in the coffee the same!

Riddle 11: Mailing a Valuable Object

Let's say you need to send your friend a mail with a valuable object in it. You have a nice box which is big enough to hold that object.

The box you have has a locking ring which is large enough to have a lock attached, and you have several locks with its matching keys.

The catch is, your friend does not have the key to any of the lock which you have. You can't send the key in an unlocked box because it can be stolen or be copied.

How are you going to safely send the valuable object while still locked to your friend?

Answer: Send your box with a lock attached to it. Your friend will attach his own lock and send the box back to you.

Upon receiving, remove your lock and send it back to your friend. Your friend may then remove the lock he put on and open the box.

Riddle 12: The Prisoner

A prisoner was told by the police, "If you tell a lie, we will hang you, but if you tell a fact, we will shoot you."

What can he say to save himself?

Answer: You will hang me.

Riddle 13: Four Fruits

In a contest in a barrio, a red apple, an orange, a banana, and a pear, have been inserted inside four secured boxes, where there is one fruit per box.

The crowd needs to guess which fruit is in

which box. One hundred twenty-three people had participated in this contest.

When the boxes were opened lately, 43 people turn out to wrongly guess all of the fruits; 39 people got one of the fruit right; and lastly, 31 people got two fruits correctly.

How many people have guessed the three fruits correctly, and how many people have guessed four fruits correctly?

Answer: It is impossible to guess only three fruits correctly, by which the fourth fruit is then correct too!

So, nobody from the participants had guessed the three fruits correctly, and 123-43-39-31 = 10 people have guessed four fruits correctly.

Riddle 14: Getting Around

A student rides on his scooter to get to the train station and arrive at school.

His house is close to two stops; the first one is a mile from home, and the second one is two miles from home in the opposite direction.

In the morning, he always gets on at the first stop while in the afternoon, he still gets off at the second one.

Why does this so?

Answer:

The stations and the student's home are on a hill, which allows him to ride down easily with his scooter.

Riddle 15: The 24th

Alone I am the 24th, but with a friend, I am 20. Add another friend, and I am unclean. What am I?

Answer: It's the letter X

It is currently the 24th letter of in the English alphabet, and then XX, when counted in Roman numerals is equals to 20, and XXX is merely a label for movies and contents that are very unclean or inappropriate.

Riddle 16: The Poison

Two girls ate dinner together one night, and they both ordered ice tea. One girl drank them very fast by which she drank five of them in the time it took the other to drink one. The girl who drank only one iced tea died while the other survived. All of the drinks were poisoned.

Why did the woman who drank more ice tea survive than the girl who drank less iced tea?

Answer: The deadly poison was in the middle of the ice. As the ice melts down, the poison becomes more visible and will be mixed into the iced tea.

Riddle 17: The Paradox of the Barber

An isolated town only has one barber, a male barber. The barber only shaves all the people who do not shave themselves.

So, who shaves the barber?

Answer: This is an example of a paradox.

If the barber shaves himself, then the second sentence would be false because he only shaves those who do not shave themselves.

If he does not shave himself, then it must be parallel to the second statement that he must shave himself.

Riddle 18: The Boys in a Circle

One day, a man was walking through the park when he saw a group of four boys standing on a circle. Then, a smaller boy is holding a large stick and hands it to a larger boy saying, "I couldn't do it, your turn."

The larger boy swung the stick twice, and the other two boys went to the ground. The smaller boy said to the three other boys, "I'll get them next time." The man walks away smiling.

What just happened?

Answer:

The boys were at a birthday party, and they were hitting a piñata.

Riddle 19: The Invisible

We can hurt without moving. We can poison without touching. We can bear the truth and also the lies. We cannot be judged by our size. What are we?

Answer: Words

Riddle 20: The Two Coconuts

Suppose you have two coconuts and you want to find out how high these coconuts can be dropped from a 100-story building before the coconuts shatter. However, you only got $1.40, and the elevator fee costs a dime each ride up (it's free for trips down).

How will you drop the coconuts to be able to guarantee that you will figure out the lowest level of floor they will shatter at while beginning your journey and ending at floor 1?

They will break when dropped from the same height and they will not weaken from getting dropped.

Answer: You can drop the coconut on floor 1 first because you start on the first floor. Then you can go to the floors: 14, 27, 39, 50, 60, 69, 77, 84, 90, 95, 99, and 100.

Whatever floor your first coconut breaks at, climb to the floor above the most recent floor the coconut didn't shatter and let go the second coconut starting from this floor level.

Then you need to climb up one floor until your second coconut shatters, and that is the lowest possible floor the coconut will break at.

///

Riddle 21: The Restless Fly

Two cyclists one day began their training run, one starting from Los Angeles and the other beginning from Texas.

When the riders were 180 miles apart from each other, a fly took an interest to them. Starting on one of the cyclists' shoulder, the fly flew ahead to meet the other cyclist. After reaching him, the fly then turned around and went back to the first one.

The restless insect continued to fly back and forth until the pair met, then settled on the nose of one rider. The fly's speed was 30 mph. Each cyclist speed was 15 mph.

How many miles did the fly travel?

Answer: The cyclists took 6 hours to meet. The fly traveled 6·30=180 miles.

Riddle 22: The Manhole

Why are manholes round instead of being a square?

Answer: If they are round, the covers in the manhole won't fall into the hole if it is slightly smaller than the cover, but if they are square, the hole would have to be about 50% of the area of the cover to stop it from falling into the hole diagonally.

Riddle 23: The Mother

The mother is 21 years older than her newborn child. In 6 years after, the mother will become 5 times older than her baby.

Where is the father?

Answer:

He is with the mother.

If you do the math equation: (baby's age) + 21 (baby's age + 6)

(baby's age) + 27 = 30 + 5 (baby's age)

-3 = 4 (baby's age)

-3/4 = baby's age

The baby is going to be born in 9 months.

Riddle 24: The Teacher's Quiz

A teacher one day decides to give her students pop quiz, but all of her students refuse to take it because they thought that the teacher would call off the quiz.

She can give only one detention to a student on her class for skipping the quiz. Each student knows each other's names, and if a student knows that he/she is getting detention, they will take the pop quiz.

How can she threaten her students with a single detention so they will all take the quiz?

Answer: She will tell them that she will give the student who skips the quiz a detention whose name comes first alphabetically.

This student won't skip it because they knew that they are getting a detention if they do.
The next person alphabetically will know then that they will get a detention so that they won't skip either, and so on. So, they will all take the pop quiz prepared by their teacher.

If you hit someone, they are out, and they no longer get a turn.

If the sequence of throwing is you, then John, and then Tom; what should you do to win the game?

Answer: You must miss the first time on purpose.

If you try to hit John, do it. Tom goes after, and he's gonna hit you, and you will lose for sure.

If you're gonna aim at Tom and hit him, then John will shoot to you. If you miss your shot on your first turn, John will go for Tom for sure because he has higher accuracy.

If he hits him, then it will be just you and John, but you are going first to him. If he misses John then Tom will hit him, and it will be just you and Tom, but then again, in this case, you're going first.

Riddle 31: A King's Name!

Five hundred is at my ending and my beginning, yet 5 is at my heart. The first letter and the first number makes me so complete.

My name is that of a king.

What am I?

Answer:

DAVID. D=500, V=5, and I=1 in Roman numerals (the first number). 'A' is the very first letter of the alphabet.

Riddle 32: The Sherlock Holmes Riddle - How Did the Women Die?

The British Police inspected a room where there are no windows, no doors, no tables and is almost empty, except there is just a puddle of water.

They found a dead person who apparently hung himself from the ceiling, but they weren't sure how it happened.

Sherlock and Bobby entered and quickly solved the case. How did the person die?

Answer:

She hung herself using huge ice slabs, which then now melted later and formed a puddle of water.

Riddle 33: Untiring Donkey

A donkey travels the exact same distance daily.

Strangely, 2 of his legs travel 40 kilometers and the remaining two travels 41 kilometers.

Obviously, two front donkey legs cannot be a 1km ahead of the hind legs.

The donkey is perfectly normal. So how come this be true?

Answer: The donkey was walking on a circular path. Thus, its outside legs travel more distance than its inner legs!

Riddle 34: Prison Break

Two prisoners, Phil Evans and Michael Stevens, were locked in a prison cell. There is an open window approximately 30 feet above the ground, and they knew that they would never be able to reach it.

They plan to escape by their man-made tunnel so they started to dig it out.

After digging for more than 20 days, Stevens comes with another plan and they successfully escaped.

What was the plan?

Answer: They use the dirt and bricks from their man-made tunnel, and stand on the pile then one on top of the other.

Riddle 35: Logical Interview Riddle

Can you divide numbers ranging 1 to 9 into two groups, so that the sum of the numbers of each group is equal?

Note: Nine cannot be turned upside down to make it a 6.

Answer: 1 2 3 4 5 9 and 7 8 9

The sum of numbers 1 2 3 4 5 6 7 8 9 is 45, so numbers can't be split into 2 equal parts.

I know I can't turn 9 upsides down and make it 6, but I can turn 6 to make it 9.

Riddle 36: Logical Puzzle - Asked On Interviews!

You organized a small get-together at my home. At the party, you have a single barrel with a whiskey in it.

Suddenly, Guest 1 says, "I bet this barrel of whiskey is more than half full."

"No, it's less than half full," Guest 2 replied.

You don't have any measuring instrument and without removing whiskey from it, how can you determine which of your guest is right?

Answer: Tilt the barrel until the whiskey barely touches the lip of the barrel. If the bottom of your barrel is visible, then the whiskey is less than half full.

If the bottom of the barrel is still completely covered by the whiskey inside, then it is more than half full.

Riddle 37: System Error

There was a system error in a mailing website because the passwords of some clients got changed.

Here is an email conversation of a client and the mailing-website response person.
Client: My password is altered.

Client: I am not able to logged-in.

Executive: The password is distinct this time, and it got eight letters, out of which two are some of your previous password.

Client: Thanks! Now I can log in.

What are the client's old and new password?

Answer:

Old password: "Distinct," New Password: "Altered."

Riddle 38: Clock Puzzle

How many times in each day, minutes and hour clock comes in a straight line?

Answer: 44

In 12 hours, the minute and the hour hands will overlap or are in exactly opposite directions 22 times.

In 24 hours, the hands will again overlap or are in the opposite direction in 44 times.

Riddle 39: The Apple Tree

I have an apple tree, by which the number of apple in this tree get doubled every week.

On 30th week, the tree gets completely filled with apples.

Can you tell me; on what week does the tree I cared so much is half covered with apples?

Answer: On the 29th week!

Riddle 40: Strange Murder

A girl met a guy at the funeral of her mother, but she did not know him. She fell to the guy and just kept looking at him the entire time.

Sometime later, it got to her that the guy is gone, and she forgot to take his number, and now she can't find him.

A few weeks later, the girl murdered her elder brother.

What is her motive in killing her own brother?

Answer: She wished that the guy would again appear at the funeral if she killed another relative, his elder brother.

Riddle 41: Next 3 Letters

What will be the next 3 letters in this riddle?

"O" – "T" – "T" – "F" – "F" – "S" – "S" _ _ _

Answer: "E-N-T" They represent the first letter when writing the numbers from One to Ten.

Riddle 42: Probability Riddle Loaded Revolver

Ben has been caught stealing livestock, and he was then brought into the town for justice.

The judge is his ex-girlfriend, Gretchen, by which wants to show him some sympathy, but the law clearly gives for two shots to be taken at Henry from the close range.

To make things a little better and comfortable for Ben himself, Gretchen tells him that she will place two bullets in a six-chambered revolver in successive order.

She will spin the chamber randomly, close it, and take one shot. If Ben is still alive from the shot, she will then either take another shot, or spin the chamber again before shooting.

Ben is a bit anxious that his own ex-girlfriend would carry out the punishment, and a bit frustrated that she was always a follower of the law.

He straightens himself as Gretchen loads the chamber, spins the revolver, and pulls the trigger. Phew! It was blank.

Then Gretchen asks, Want me to pull the trigger again, or should I spin the chamber again before pulling the trigger?'

What must Ben choose on what Gretchen said?

Answer: Ben should have let Gretchen pull the trigger again without spinning it.

We know that Gretchen fired one of the four empty chambers. Since the bullets were placed in the consecutive order, one of the empty chambers is followed by a bullet, and so the three remaining empty chambers are followed by another empty chamber.

So, if Henry tells Gretchen to pull the trigger once again, the probability that a bullet will be fired from the gun is 1/4.

If Gretchen will spin the chamber again, the probability that she shoots Henry is gonna be 1/3 or

2/3 since there are two possible bullets that would be in firing position.

Riddle 43: Alexander Puzzle

Alexander was stranded on an isolated island covered in forest.

One day, when a strong wind is blowing from the west side, lightning struck the west end of the island and fire started to get ablaze to the forest.

The fire was very massive, burning everything in its every path, and if he did nothing, the fire would burn the whole island immediately, killing him in the process.

Cliffs are surrounding the island, so he can't jump off and get away from the fire. How will the Alexander survive the forest fire on the island?

Note: There are no buckets or any other means to put out the fire.

Answer:

Alexander will pick up a piece of wood and lights it using the fire on the west end of the island.

He quickly moves it near the east end of the islands and starts a new fire. The wind from the west will cause that fire to burn out the eastern end, and he can now then shelter in the burnt area.

Alexander may survive the fire, but he will die because of starvation, with all the food in the forest burnt because of the fire caused by lightning.

Riddle 44: Crime Puzzle

There is a certain crime which is punishable if attempted, but if it is committed, is not. What crime is this?

Answer: Suicide

///

Riddle 45: Murder Mystery Humor

A donkey behind another donkey.

I'm behind that second donkey.

But there's a whole nation behind me.

The word is hugely related to a murder case!

Answer: Ass-ass-i-nation "Assassination."

///

Riddle 46: What Is Ben Buying?

Ben went to a hardware store and asked a

54

staff for the price of some items. The salesman said: One costs $1, eight costs $1, seventeen cost $2, One hundred four costs $3, One thousand seventy-two costs $4.

What was Ben buying?

Answer: Ben was buying home address numbers, and they cost $1 per digit!

Riddle 47: Romantic

What's the most romantic thing about the ocean?

Answer: When the buoy meets gull!

Riddle 48: The Man with Seven Wives

On my way to St. Ives, I saw a man with his 7 wives. Each wife had 7 sacks.

Each of that sack had 7 cats. Each cat had

their 7 kittens. Kitten, cats, sacks, wives. How many, all in all, were going to St. Ives?

Answer: One, only me.

Riddle 49: World's Most Famous Riddle

What came first, the chicken or the egg?

Answer: Dinosaurs laid eggs long before there were chickens in the Earth! The riddle didn't mention what type of egg.

Riddle 50: November

A man sitting near the seashore is feeling rather poor. He then saw the man next to him pull a wad of $50 notes out of his wallet.

He then turns to the rich man and says to him,

'I have a great talent; I know almost every song that has ever existed and played.'

The rich man laughs.

The poor man countered, 'I am willing to bet you all of that money you have in your wallet. I can definitely sing an original song with a lady's name of your choice in it.'

The rich man laughed again and asked, 'Okay, how about you sing a song with my daughter's name, Joanna Armstrong-Miller?'

The poor man sang a song. The rich man goes home poor. The poor man goes home rich.

What song did he sing?

Answer: Happy Birthday

Riddle 51: UPSC Interview Question

The Bay of Bengal is in which state?

Answer: Liquid :-)

Riddle 52: Another UPSC Interview Riddle

How can a man survive 20 days without sleep?

Answer:

No Problem, He sleeps at night!

Riddle 53: A Brilliant Student's Puzzle

There was once a university that offered a class on Probability that they can apply to the real world.

The class may seem very easy, but there

was a catch. There were no homework assignments or tests, or even activities, but there was a final exam that would contain only a single question on it.

When everyone received the test, it was only a blank sheet of paper with a tricky question on it: 'What is a risk?'

Most students passed, but only a single student had received a 100% score for the class!

Even stranger was he only wrote down one word in his paper!

What did he write?

Answer: The brilliant student wrote down: "This."

Riddle 54: IPS Interview Riddle

If you had four oranges and three apples on your left hand and four apples and three oranges in your right hand, what do you have?

Answer: Very large hands.

Riddle 55: Sound Riddle

Can you figure out the logic that was used to decide the order of the following words?

Gun - shoe - spree - door - hive - kicks - heaven - gate - line - den

Answer: Each word rhymes with the sound of the numbers starting from "one"... (One = Gun)

Riddle 56: Puzzle for Math Wizs!

Using only eight eights and the power of addition, how can you make 1000?

Answer: 1000 = 888 + 88 + 8 + 8 + 8

Riddle 57: Hardly There

I'm a word that's hardly there. Take away my beginning, and I become an herbal flair. What am I?

Answer: Sparsely (No S = Parsley)!

Riddle 58: Air Ballooning

One sunny afternoon, three wise men went for a ride on a hot air balloon over the Sahara Desert.

An hour later into the trip, the balloon began to lose its altitude. A month later, a random person found one of the ballooners lying on the desert sand dead, naked, and holding half a toothpick. What happened to him?

Answer: As the balloon lost altitude, the men took off their clothes and threw them overboard to decrease the weight of the balloon.

The balloon didn't stop dropping, so the men decided to draw straws to see who will jump first.

The dead man drew the shortest stick (the half toothpick).

Riddle 59: Rebus Puzzle for Kids

What does this mean: T RN?

Answer: No U-turn (think about the word "turn")

Riddle 60: Fun Math Puzzle

Baseball bat and ball cost $50. If the bat costs $49 more than the ball, what is the cost of each?

Answer:

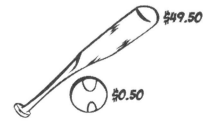

$49.50

$0.50

Bat $49.50, Ball $0.50

Riddle 61: White and black balls

The first box has two red balls. The second box has two blue balls. The third box has a red and a blue ball.

The boxes are labeled, but all labels are wrong!

You are only allowed to undo one box, then draw a ball from the box you chose at random, look at its color and put it back into the same box without looking at the color of the other ball on that box.

How many times do you need to repeat this process for you to be able to label the boxes correctly?

Answer: Just One!

Because you know all labels are wrong, you can solve this by following this same logic rule.

The "BR" ("BR" stands for Blue - Red) box must be either BB (All Blue) or RR (All Red).

Selecting one ball from the "BR" box will definitely let you know which.

You can then solve the other two boxes correctly as

long as you follow the logic that the labels "are ALL LABELLED WRONG" initially!

Riddle 62: Rectangles

Draw four rectangles on a piece of paper. Put nine X's in the four rectangles so that there are no same number of X's in each rectangle.

Answer:

Draw one large rectangle. Next, draw three smaller rectangles inside the large rectangle.

Place three X's in each small rectangle. There will certainly be nine X's in the large rectangle.

Riddle 63: Metal Washer Ring

While playing with a metal washer that was shaped like a ring, Dave accidentally pushed it on his finger too far and now couldn't get it off.

He tries to remove it using soap and water, but it didn't work. The hospital sent him to a specific service station thinking they could cut the metal that was stuck. Since the ring was made with specially hardened steel, it couldn't be cut easily.

Just then Phil arrived on the scene and suggested the people an easy way to remove the washer on Dave's finger in just a few minutes. What was his solution?

Answer: Bob suggested that Dave will hold his finger in the air while someone will wound a piece of string firmly around his finger just above the metal ring. The string forced the swelling down.

As they unwounded the string from the nearest end of the ring, someone else will inserted the ring up.

They must continue winding and unwinding the string until the metal ring could be easily removed.

Riddle 64: Does an Elephant Fit Inside a Refrigerator?

How can you fit an elephant inside a refrigerator? How you fit a Giraffe inside a refrigerator?

The Lion is throwing a party and invited all the animals in the jungle. All of them came except for one. Which animal is it?

You come across a lake which is a home for huge crocodiles. You can't walk around it, you can't swim under the water, and you can't even jump or swing over it!

How do you get across the lake?

Answer:

A. You open the door, put the elephant inside the refrigerator and close the door.

B. You need to OPEN the door, take the elephant out of the fridge, put the giraffe inside, and then close the door.

C. The Giraffe because he's still inside the refrigerator

D. You can swim through the lake peacefully since all the crocodile is currently at the party!

Riddle 65: Come as a Punch

I can come in a can,

I can come as a punch,

I can come as a win,

You can eat me for lunch.

What am I?

Answer: Beet/Beat

Riddle 66: Twins' Birthday

Peter celebrated his birthday one day, and 2 days later his older twin brother, Paul, celebrated his own birthday.

How could this happen?

Answer: When their mother was about to give birth, she and her husband were travelling by boat.

The older sibling, Paul, was born first on March 1st.

After the boat crossed a time zone, the younger sibling was born. His birthday was February 28th!

During leap years, the younger sibling celebrates his birthday two days right before the older sibling!

Riddle 67: Car Ride!

Assumingly you are a mother of 5 kids and got to try to get them all into the car at once.

Timmy and Tommy are twins, but they really hate each other so they can't go together and Sarah and Sally hate each other too, so they can't go together, and Max is gay so he's only able to sit by the guys and there are only 5 seats.

You need to put them in the correct order

68

inside the car, so everyone feels happy during the trip...

Answer:

Sarah, Tommy, Max, Timmy, and then Sally

Riddle 68: Sherlock Holmes Murder Mystery Riddle

Sherlock breaks into a crime scene.

The victim is slumped dead on his chair and has a bullet hole in his head.

A gun was laying in the floor alongside a cassette recorder beneath the table. Upon pressing the play button, Holmes heard the message, 'I have committed sins in my life, and now I am offering my soul to the lord" and followed by a gunshot.

Sherlock smiled and informed the police that's it's a murder. Why did he think so?

Answer: There's no way for the dead victim to rewind the tape himself!

Riddle 69: Tricky Logical Mind Bender

A man was looking through the window of the 44th floor of a building. He surprisingly opened the window lock and jumped on the other side of the window.

Upon hitting the floor, the man received no injury.

How is the man okay if he didn't even have a parachute?

Answer: The man is a regular window cleaner who went inside the window after finishing off his job on the 44th floor.

Riddle 70: Awesome Idea Puzzle Problem

Along with Vin Diesel, Dwayne Johnson was running away with a bag of money from a heist in their car...

One tire was punctured, so he dropped down to replace it. While replacing the wheel, he accidentally dropped the four nuts that were holding the wheel, and they fell into a drain.

Vin Diesel gave him an idea using which they were able to drive until the rendezvous point.

What was the idea?

Answer:

ONE NUT PER WHEELS!

Vin Diesel told him to put one of the nuts from each of the other wheels.

Riddle 71: Doorbells in Egypt

Why do Egyptian pyramids have doorbells?

Answer: So you toot-'n'-come-in.

Riddle 72: That's Confusing

The answer most people give to this question is "Yes," but what all of them mean is "No."

What's the question?

Answer: Do you mind?

Riddle 73: Getting Away with Murder

Two cars got involved in an accident.
The man who was driving a tiny red car
overtook a big black car.

The driver of the red car didn't notice the

oncoming traffic, and so he had to swerve back in, causing the big black car to swerve uncontrollably and crash into a shop window.

When the occupants of both cars were checked, everyone in the red car was okay, but in the black car, one of the passengers was already dead man.

However, the driver of the red car was not charged with manslaughter, murder, or any similar criminal liability!

Why was this so?

Answer:

The black car was actually a hearse and was really on its way to a funeral!

Riddle 74: Google Interview Puzzle

On a faraway village, 7 brothers live in a house on their own. And without electricity or internet whatsoever, these are what they do most of the time:

Brother-1: Reading books

Brother-2: Cooking food

Brother-3: Playing Chess

Brother-4: Playing Sudoku

Brother-5: Washing clothes

Brother-6: Gardening

What is Sister-7 doing?

Answer: He's playing Chess. Chess usually need 2 players!

Riddle 75: Crime Scene Logic Puzzle

A dead body suddenly fell outside a 10-story building which had no rooftop. The best police detective is called to look at the scene.

From the initial position of the body, the early reports said that the victim committed suicide.

But the detective knew something is wrong.

He went to the first floor of the building and then walked to the direction where the dead body outside is, then he opened the window and tossed a penny outside.

He was able to do this to all 10 floors of the building. The baffled police officers at the ground floor were just baffled by the actions of the detective.

Then he came down and told his guys it was a murder. How in heaven did the detective deduce that?

Answer: When he was throwing the coins outside the window of each floor, what he was really doing was checking if the windows were initially closed or open.

And since he had to open up all the windows on all 10 floors, he knew that it was a murder because if the victim committed suicide, then there should be at least 1 window open.

Riddle 76: The Man in the Elevator

A mysterious man who hates walking always take the elevator from his apartment on the 10th floor down to the ground floor to go to work or to go shopping.

However, when he comes back up again, he always stops on the 7th floor and climbs up the stairs to his apartment.

Why is he climbing from the 7th floor to his apartment?

Answer: The man is (of course) a short person. He can't reach the 10th-floor button although he wants to!

Riddle 77: Death in a Field

A mysterious man is lying dead in a field. On his back is an unopened backpack. There is no other animal or person in the area. How did the man die?

Answer: The man jumped out of a plane, but his parachute failed to open.

Riddle 78: The Coal, Carrot, and Scarf

A carrot, an old hat, and a scarf are lying on a lawn. Someone put them on the lawn, but there is a perfectly logical reason why they chose those things to put on the lawn.

What is it?

Answer: It was a snowman before! The kids made a snowman the other day and forgot to fetch the stuff they used.

This riddle is called a "State Puzzle," and you should definitely be more aware of this kind because there are more coming your way!

Riddle 79: The Trouble with Having Sons!

A woman was giving birth, and 2 boys went out off of her at the same day, at the same hour, at the same year.

However, they are not twins. Why is that?

Answer: She gave birth to a set of triplets!

Riddle 80: Push that Car!

An old man was pushing his car all the way until he stopped at a hotel because he knew he was already bankrupt.

What is he doing?

Answer: He was playing Monopoly.

Riddle 81: The Arm of the Postal Service

One peaceful day, an old man received a parcel in his mail. Carefully packed, inside the parcel was a human arm.

He looked at it, smiled as if he remembered something, repacked and then sent it away on to another old man.

The second man also carefully looked at the arm before taking it to the woods and burying it. Why did they do this?

Answer: Three men were once stranded on an uninhabited island with no food. Out of desperation, the three men who were very close friends agreed to cut off their left arms one by one in order to have food.

The first man and the second man had to amputate

their arms for food, until one day before the third man had to cut off his arms, help arrived, and all of them got rescued.

To keep his promise to his friends, the third man still kept his word and went to the doctor and amputated his arm.

He was then the one who sent the parcel to those men who, for a very long time, had been carrying the memories of an experience they will never forget.

Riddle 82: Heaven

A young man died and went to straight to Heaven. There were millions of other people there. They were all naked, and all looked young as they did at the age of 21.

He looked around the place to greet and to see if he could find someone he knew. He then suddenly saw a couple, and he knew instantly that they were Adam and Eve without even knowing how they looked when they were alive!

How did he know?

Answer: He recognized them because he saw that they were the only people there without belly buttons!

Because both of them were not born of women, they never had umbilical cords, and therefore they never had a belly button.

This one, however, might start off some vicious theological arguments when used!

Riddle 83: The Pear Tree Dude

A farmer and his beautiful pear tree once supplied fruits to a local supermarket.

The shop owner called up the farmer to know how many fruits are available for him to buy that day. The farmer knew from his memory that the main trunk has 24 branches. Each branch has exactly 12 stems in it, and each stem has exactly 10 twigs, and each twig has one piece of fruit in it.

All in all, how many plums will the farmer be able to deliver?

Answer:

None – what he had was pears!

Riddle 84: What is the Day?

If the name of the day after the day before yesterday was Tuesday, and the name of the day before the day after tomorrow is Thursday, what day is today?

Answer: Wednesday (this one will make your friend's brain hurt!)

Riddle 85: The School Pupils

At a local office, 27 employees wore red coats, 29 employees wore black coats, and 40 employees wore blue coats. How many employees were wearing green coats?

Answer: 49 employees!

The letter A = 1, B = 2, C is equal to 3 and so forth, so GREEN = 7 + 18 + 5 + 5 + 14 = 49

Riddle 86: The Man and the Beaker

A 6-foot tall lady was holding a glass bowl above her head. She let it drop to the carpet without spilling a single drop of soup.

How could she manage to drop the glass from a height of six feet and not spill a drop of soup?

Answer: The glass bowl was empty.

Riddle 87: Jane and Jill

Bobby gave Bill the following challenge: "If you sit down in that chair, I bet you five dollars I can make you get out of it before I run around the chair three times," he said.

"That isn't fair," Bill said. "You'll just tickle me with or something."

"Nope," Bobby said. "I won't even touch you, either with an object or directly. You can only get out of it by your own decision."

Bill thought that it was just fair, accepted the challenge, sat on the chair, and two minutes later, he got up. Bobby won the bet.

How did he do it?

Answer: Bill sat down in the chair. Bobby ran around it twice, then he said, "I'll be back in two weeks to run the third time around!

Riddle 88: What Can't You hold?

What things can you hold using your right hand, but not in your left?

Answer:

Your left forearm hand, or elbow!

Riddle 89: An Arab Sheikh

An Arab billionaire tells his two sons to race their camels to a very distant city to see who will inherit his fortune.

There is one twist though, the one whose camel is slower will win.

So the billionaire went on his plane and flew to

the distant city to see who will win.

After wandering aimlessly for weeks, the brothers got so tired of the rules of the race.

They took a break and asked a wise man for guidance. Upon receiving his advice, they quickly jumped on the camels and raced to the city as quickly as they can to win the fortune.

What was the wise man's advice?

Answer: He told them to switch camels!

Riddle 90: The Philosopher's Clock

An absent-minded ancient philosopher didn't correctly wind up his big clock hanging on the wall after he replaced the battery. He had no radio, internet, TV, telephone or any other means for telling the correct time.

So, he traveled on foot to a friend's place a few miles down the desert road. He knew it was a 2-hour walk to get to his friend's house so he tried his best not get distracted along the way.

When he got there, he said hi and then he came back home knowing the correct time to put in his clock.

How did he do it?

Answer: Clocks measure time length even when they do not show the correct time.

As long as he knew how much his travel time is going to be back and forth to his friend's house and the initial time displayed on his wrongly winded clock on his home, he could do it.

His friend had a clock on his home, and he wrote down what time it is on his friend's clock, and he went on his way home to correct his time by subtracting his journey time he used to walk to his friend's house and return to his own house.

Riddle 91: The Three Palefaces

Three young men were taken captive by a hostile tribe. And according to their tribe's rule, if they want to be free, they had to answer the tribe's intelligence test first.

The tribe's chief showed them 5 headbands - 3 white and 2 red. The 3 young men's eyes were then covered, and lined up with each other, all facing the other one's back like a line in the grocery store.

The chief then attached a headband on each of their heads while they were still blindfolded, hid the two headbands which remained, and pulled out all of each man's eye cover.

So, the third young man could see the color of headbands attached to the two young men standing in front of him, the second young man could see the color of the headband of the first young man, and the first could not see any of the headbands from his position.

And by the rules, if any one of the three young men could determine (or guess) the color of his own headband correctly, they all go home, and they win their freedom. If not, the tribe will make them their slaves.

It so happened that all 3 young men were prominent students from a local academy. and after just 5 minutes, the first man, (the one in front) shouted:

"The color of my headband is ..."

What color did he say and why?

Answer:

The first one (although he didn't see any of the other headbands) thought like this:

The man at the last of the line is silent, which only means, he doesn't have a way to know his color. Therefore, at least one of the headbands he's seeing in front of him is white.

Because if both of us in front of him would be red, then he would know that his headband is white because there are only two red headbands. However, he is silent, so he doesn't know what color is his headband.

My pal in the middle is very silent too. So he knows that one of us it white though because he also knew that the third guy would've already spoken up if the middle and I one is wearing red.

If I was wearing a red headband, the second one would have known that he had a white headband because there are only 2 red headbands, and again, if the middle one and I wore red, we would have been saved long ago. However, nobody dares to speak up, so my headband is not red – my headband is white.

Riddle 92: The Bobber

You can consistently paddle your canoe seven miles per hour through any calm lake. The stream you're fishing at flows at three miles per hour.

One of a fisherman's bobbers broke in the water fourteen miles upstream of you and is now being carried by the current downstream.

How many hours will you need to meet the bobber if you paddle upstream?

Answer: Forget about the speed of the stream, because both you and the bobber will get carried by the stream three miles per hour.

Just use your paddle speed and compute. It will take two hours to paddle 14 miles with your rate of seven miles per hour.

Riddle 93: The Socks

Bobby has twelve gray socks and twelve black socks in his drawer.

Without looking and in complete darkness, how many socks must he randomly take from the drawer in order to make sure to get a pair that matches color?

Answer: Socks don't come in left and right pairs, so any gray will pair with any other gray, and any black sock will pair with any other black.

So he just needs three socks. If he has three socks and they are either colored gray or black, then he will get at least a pair of sock of the same color, giving him one matching pair!

Riddle 94: The Great Dilemma

On a very wild and stormy night, you are driving down the road with your 2-seater car when you drive by a local bus stop, and you see the three people waiting for the bus, which are:

1. A very old lady who looks very weak

2. An old pal whom you did all sorts of crazy stuff with

3. The perfect woman / man you've been dreaming about.

Knowing that there can only be one other passenger in your car, whom would you choose?

Answer:

The old lady of course! After helping the old lady you're your car, you're gonna give your keys to your friend so he can drive, and wait for the bus with your perfect partner.

Riddle 95: Bad Boy Lucy

Bad Boy Lucy was warned by his mother that he must never open the door of their cellar, or he will see stuff that wasn't meant for him to see. One afternoon while his mother was out, he immediately opens the cellar door.

What did he see?

Answer: When Bad Boy Lucy opened the door, he saw sunlight and their living room, and over its windows, their garden.

He had never seen any of these things before because his mother always kept and enclosed him all of his life in the cellar.

Riddle 96: The Surgeon

A man and his son got involved in a car crash. The dad was killed, and the kid was taken to the nearest hospital with critical injuries.

When he got there, the attending surgeon said, 'I don't wanna operate on this child – for he is my only son!' How can this possibly be?

Answer: The surgeon is the boy's mom!

Riddle 97: A River-y Mess

A drunk man one day was driving alone to his home in his car when he suddenly went off the road at high speed.

He crashed through the metal fence and went down a steep ravine before the car crashed and dumped into a fast-flowing river. As the car slowly sunk in the river, the man realized that both his arms were broken, and he couldn't release himself from the seatbelt to get out of the car.

The car gradually sank up to the bottom of the river, and so the man got trapped in the car. Rescuers arrived at the scene one hour later, yet they found him in the river with broken arms, but still alive.

How was he able to survive?

Answer:

The water in the river was only 4-feet deep!

Riddle 98: The Truck Driver

An on-duty police officer saw a truck driver clearly going the opposite way down a one-way street, but the cop did not try to stop him.

Why didn't he stop the truck driver?

Answer: The truck driver was just walking with some groceries!

Riddle 99: Rice

A man bought corn at $1 a pound from local growers and sells them for 3 cents a pound in a very poor country. Because of this, he became a multi-millionaire. How come?

Answer: The man was a philanthropist who bought tons of great quality of corn to sell to the poor residents at the prices that would fit their income.

He was originally a multi-billionaire, but he lost so much money in a lot for his kindness, and that made him a millionaire!

Riddle 100: The Incontrovertible Proof

A woman has a very strong proof in court that

all of her money was stolen by her sister. Both the woman and her sister, the suspect, came before the Judge.

Later on during the trial, the judge declares, "This is by far the strangest case I've ever seen. Though the woman's proof is absolutely factual, her sister before me cannot be punished."

How can this possibly be?

Answer: The sisters are conjoined twins!

Riddle 101: In a Foreign City

It was the middle of a dark and stormy night, and a young couple was in a car speeding thoroughly through a foreign country. Their car broke down because of the rain, and the husband needs to help from someone who spoke his English.

He was very afraid to leave his wife alone by herself in the car, so he pulled up all the car windows and locked the car before leaving her.

When he came back with help, the car was in the same state, as though nothing happened, but he found his wife lifeless, and there was blood all over the car floor, and there was a stranger sitting beside her wife.

What happened?

Answer:

His wife was about to give birth to their baby, and they were driving to the nearest hospital. The baby went out in the car, but his wife didn't survive.

Riddle 102: All the Left Fingers in the World

Assuming that there are approximately 8,000,000,000 people on Earth.

What would you estimate to be the answer, if you're going to multiply the number of fingers in every person's left-hands altogether?

Answer: The answer would be zero.

It will only take a single person to have no fingers on his left hand to make the product zero because any number, no matter how big, when multiplied with zero is zero.

Riddle 103: The Coconut Grove

A nightclub called 'The Coconut Grove' had a very terrible fire in the past which resulted in over 400 people to die. A very simple mechanism in the building led to the death of all these people.

Since this accident, all laws over the whole world were changed to ensure that all public buildings throughout the world would eliminate this one small detail which proved to be so deadly.

What was this detail?

Answer: The doors at 'The Coconut Grove' can only be opened inward. During the panic to escape the fire, people were got stuck against these doors and could not pull them open after people after people kept pushing on the door.

After 'The Coconut Grove' disaster in 1942, all public buildings made must have doors which opens outward.

Riddle 104: The Smuggling Boat

A man accidentally fell off from a smuggling boat into deep water. He had zero swimming skills, and he wasn't wearing anything to keep him afloat in the water.

It somehow took 30 minutes for the people on the boat to realize that a crew was missing on the personnel. The man was then rescued afterward.

Why didn't he drown in the deep water?

Answer: The boat where they were going through was the Dead Sea, whose water is so dense and so salty that anyone in it floats very easily.

Fun fact: The maximum known depth of the Dead Sea is 1,237' (377 m), and smuggling boats are well known to use the Dead Sea to transport goods.

Riddle 105: Bobby and the Photograph

Bobby was looking at a photo in his pocket.

Someone noticed him asked, "Who is that you're looking at?" He replied: "I do not have a brother or sister, but the dad of this man is my dad's son."

So, whose picture was Bobby looking at?

Answer: It was his son.

Riddle 106: Smullyan's Riddle

A young dealer bought an article for $8, sold it for $9, bought it back for $10, and sold it for $11.

How much profit did he make?

Answer:

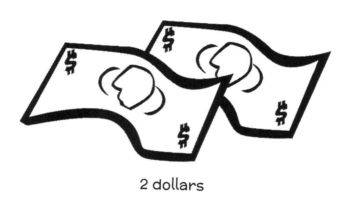

2 dollars

Riddle 107: TRAPPED

There is a room in a building with no windows, doors, or any sort of opening, and the walls are solid steel which is 10 feet thick, and you are trapped inside, left only with glue and an apple cut in half.

How will you escape the room?

Answer: You glue the apple back together to make a "WHOLE," and you crawl out through the whole (HOLE)!

WANT MORE DIFFICULT RIDDLES JUST LIKE THESE TODAY?

GO TO **AMAZON.COM** AND GET THE REST OF THE SERIES NOW!

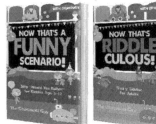 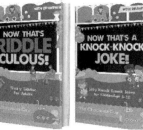 

• Now That's Riddle-Culous! Silly Riddles for Kiddos Age 5-11 (First Edition)

• Now That's A Knock-Knock Joke! Silly Knock-Knock Jokes for Kiddos Age 5-12 (Third Edition)

• Now That's A Funny Scenario! Silly "Would You Rather" Jokes for Kiddos Age 5-12 (Fourth Edition)

• Now That's A Fun Fact! Silly and Witty Random Facts for Kiddos Age 5-12 (Fifth Edition)

• Now That's A Fun Fact! More Silly and Witty Random Facts for Kiddos Age 5-12 (Sixth Edition)

• Now That's A Fun Fact! Silly and Witty Animal Facts for Kiddos Age 5-12 (Seventh Edition)

• Now That's A Fun Fact! Silly and Witty Food Facts for Kiddos Age 5-12 (Eighth Edition)

Made in the USA
Lexington, KY
07 August 2019